Business QUOTES

Enclosed in this book are quotes about the business world that have been compiled to break up the boardroom, warm up the water cooler and sweeten the pot at the coffee machine.

We hope this collection of office humor helps ease the pressures and speeds up the "nine to five" clock.

"TO ERR IS HUMAN, TO FORGIVE IS NOT COMPANY POLICY."

"SAY NO, THEN NEGOTIATE."

"IF AT FIRST YOU DON'T SUCCEED, TRY, TRY AGAIN...THEN GIVE UP. THERE'S NO USE BEING A DAMN FOOL ABOUT IT."

W.C. FIELDS

MURPHY'S LAW:

"IF ANYTHING CAN GO WRONG, IT WILL."

O'TOOLE'S COMMENTARY ON MURPHY'S LAW:

"MURPHY WAS AN OPTIMIST."

"If you don't agree with me, it means you haven't been listening."

SAM MARKEWICH

"A BILLION DOLLARS ISN'T WHAT IT USED TO BE."

NELSON BUNKER HUNT

"IF YOU CAN'T CONVINCE THEM, CONFUSE THEM."

HARRY S. TRUMAN

"AN HONEST EXECUTIVE IS ONE WHO SHARES THE CREDIT WITH THE MAN WHO DID ALL THE WORK."

"BEFORE YOU HAVE AN ARGUMENT WITH YOUR BOSS, TAKE A GOOD LOOK AT BOTH SIDES— HIS SIDE AND THE OUTSIDE."

"IT ISN'T WHAT
YOU KNOW THAT
COUNTS, IT'S
WHAT YOU THINK
OF IN TIME."

RULE OF FAILURE:

"IF AT FIRST YOU DON'T SUCCEED, DESTROY ALL EVIDENCE THAT YOU TRIED."

"AMERICA IS THE LAND OF OPPORTUNITY IF YOU'RE A BUSINESSMAN IN JAPAN."

LAWRENCE J. PETER

"NOTHING IS QUITE AS EMBARRASSING AS WATCHING YOUR BOSS DO SOMETHING YOU ASSURED HIM COULDN'T BE DONE."

"THE MARK OF A TRUE M.B.A. IS THAT HE IS OFTEN WRONG BUT SELDOM IN DOUBT."

ROBERT BUZZELL

"THERE IS NO JOB
SO SIMPLE THAT
IT CANNOT BE
DONE WRONG."

Law of destiny:

"GLORY MAY BE
FLEETING, BUT
OBSCURITY IS
FOREVER."

"A BUSINESS IS TOO BIG WHEN IT TAKES A WEEK FOR GOSSIP TO GO FROM ONE END OF THE OFFICE TO THE OTHER."

IF IT AIN'T BROKE, DON'T FIX IT— UNLESS YOU ARE A CONSULTANT."

WINTON G. ROSSITER

"THE MECHANICS OF RUNNING
A BUSINESS ARE REALLY NOT
VERY COMPLICATED WHEN YOU
GET DOWN TO ESSENTIALS. YOU
HAVE TO MAKE SOME STUFF
AND SELL IT TO SOMEBODY FOR
MORE THAN IT COST YOU.
THAT'S ABOUT ALL THERE IS
TO IT, EXCEPT FOR A FEW
MILLION DETAILS."

JOHN L. McCAFFREY

"MY DECISION IS MAYBE— AND THAT'S FINAL."

"IF IT'S DIFFICULT WE
DO IT IMMEDIATELY.
IF IT'S IMPOSSIBLE
IT TAKES A LITTLE
LONGER.

MIRACLES BY
APPOINTMENT ONLY."

"OLD SALESMEN NEVER DIE— THEY JUST GET OUT OF COMMISSION."

"A COMMITTEE IS TWELVE MEN DOING THE WORK OF ONE."

JOHN F. KENNEDY

"BUSINESS:
THE ART OF
EXTRACTING
MONEY FROM
ANOTHER MAN'S
POCKET WITHOUT
RESORTING TO
VIOLENCE."

MAX AMSTERDAM

"THE CLOSEST TO PERFECTION A PERSON EVER COMES IS WHEN HE FILLS OUT A JOB APPLICATION FORM."

STANLEY J. RANDALL

"THE TROUBLE
WITH MIXING
BUSINESS AND
PLEASURE IS THAT
PLEASURE USUALLY
COMES OUT ON
TOP."

"BLESSED ARE THE YOUNG, FOR THEY SHALL INHERIT THE NATIONAL DEBT."

HERBERT HOOVER

"NEVER TELL A LIE...UNLESS LYING IS ONE OF YOUR STRONG POINTS."

GEORGE WASHINGTON PLUNKETT

"MARKETING IS SIMPLY SALES WITH A COLLEGE EDUCATION."

JOHN FREUND

"A GOOD BUSINESS MANAGER HIRES OPTIMISTS AS SALESMEN AND PESSIMISTS TO RUN THE CREDIT DEPARTMENT."

"NO BUSINESS OPPORTUNITY IS EVER LOST. IF YOU FUMBLE IT, YOUR COMPETITOR WILL FIND IT."

"DOING BUSINESS WITHOUT ADVERTISING IS LIKE WINKING AT A GIRL IN THE DARK. YOU KNOW WHAT YOU'RE DOING, BUT NOBODY ELSE DOES."

STEWART BRITT

"OCTOBER. THIS IS ONE OF THE PECULIARLY DANGEROUS MONTHS TO SPECULATE IN STOCKS. THE OTHERS ARE JULY, JANUARY, SEPTEMBER, APRIL, NOVEMBER, MAY, MARCH, JUNE, DECEMBER, AUGUST AND FEBRUARY."

MARK TWAIN

"BUSINESS IS LIKE AN AUTOMOBILE. IT WON'T RUN ITSELF, EXCEPT DOWNHILL."

"IT'S NOT WHETHER YOU WHETHER YOU WIN OR LOSE— IT'S HOW YOU PLACE THE BLAME."

Rule of Success:

"TRUST ONLY THOSE
WHO STAND TO
LOSE AS MUCH
AS YOU WHEN
THINGS GO WRONG."

"IF PEOPLE LISTENED TO THEMSELVES MORE OFTEN, THEY WOULD TALK LESS."

"SOME EXECUTIVES CALL PASSING THE BUCK DELEGATING AUTHORITY."

THE GOLDEN RULE:

"HE WHO HAS THE GOLD MAKES THE RULES."

"IF YOU PICK UP A
STARVING DOG AND
MAKE HIM PROSPEROUS,
HE WILL NOT BITE YOU.

THIS IS THE PRINCIPAL
DIFFERENCE BETWEEN A
DOG AND A MAN."

MARK TWAIN

"A SUCCESSFUL EXECUTIVE IN BUSINESS IS ONE WHO CAN DELEGATE ALL THE RESPONSIBILITY, SHIFT ALL THE BLAME, AND APPROPRIATE ALL THE CREDIT."

"WHEN I FIRST STARTED WORKING I USED TO DREAM OF THE DAY WHEN I MIGHT BE EARNING THE SALARY I'M STARVING ON NOW."

"ANYONE WHO THINKS THE CUSTOMER ISN'T IMPORTANT SHOULD TRY DOING WITHOUT HIM FOR A PERIOD OF NINETY DAYS."

"THE TYPICAL SALESMAN IS A MAN WITH A SMILE ON HIS FACE, A SHINE ON HIS SHOES, AND A LOUSY TERRITORY."

"HAPPINESS IS A POSITIVE CASH FLOW."

FRED ADLER

"THE BEST WAY
TO APPRECIATE
YOUR JOB IS TO
IMAGINE YOURSELF
WITHOUT ONE."

THINGS THAT CAN BE COUNTED ON:

MARKETING........................ SAYS YES

FINANCE............................... SAYS NO

LEGAL.................................... HAS TO REVIEW IT

PERSONNEL........................... IS CONCERNED

PLANNING............................ IS FRANTIC

ENGINEERING....................... IS ABOVE IT ALL

MANUFACTURING............. WANTS MORE
FLOOR SPACE

TOP MANAGEMENT........... WANTS SOMEONE
RESPONSIBLE

"AN EFFICIENT BUSINESSMAN WHO FOUND A MACHINE THAT WOULD DO HALF HIS WORK, BOUGHT TWO."

"A NICKEL GOES A LONG WAY NOW. YOU CAN CARRY IT AROUND FOR DAYS WITHOUT FINDING A THING IT WILL BUY."

"THERE ARE
SOME MEN WHO,
IN A FIFTY-FIFTY
PROPOSITION,
INSIST ON
GETTING THE
HYPHEN TOO."

LAWRENCE J. PETER

"IF YOU WANT SOMETHING DONE, GIVE IT TO A BUSY MAN...AND HE'LL HAVE HIS SECRETARY DO IT."

"THERE IS NOTHING MORE DEMORALIZING THAN A SMALL BUT ADEQUATE INCOME."

EDMUND WILSON

"AMONG THE CHIEF WORRIES OF TODAY'S BUSINESS EXECUTIVES IS THE LARGE NUMBER OF UNEMPLOYED STILL ON THE PAYROLLS."

"HARD WORK IS THE YEAST THAT RAISES THE DOUGH."

"IT IS ESPECIALLY HARD TO WORK FOR MONEY YOU'VE ALREADY SPENT FOR SOMETHING YOU DIDN'T NEED."

"COMMITTEE WORK IS LIKE A SOFT CHAIR—EASY TO GET INTO BUT HARD TO GET OUT OF."

"IF ALL THE ECONOMISTS IN THE WORLD WERE LAID END TO END, IT WOULD PROBABLY BE A GOOD THING."

"CHOOSE A JOB YOU LOVE, AND YOU WILL NEVER HAVE TO WORK A DAY IN YOUR LIFE."

CONFUCIUS

"I'M OPPOSED TO
MILLIONAIRES,
BUT IT WOULD
BE DANGEROUS
TO OFFER ME
THE POSITION."

MARK TWAIN

"IDEALISM INCREASES IN DIRECT PROPORTION TO ONE'S DISTANCE FROM THE PROBLEM."

JOHN GALSWORTHY

"I CANNOT GIVE YOU A FORMULA FOR SUCCESS, BUT I CAN GIVE YOU THE FORMULA FOR FAILURE: TRY TO PLEASE EVERYBODY."

HERBERT SWOPE

"THERE ARE THREE
KINDS OF LIES:

LIES,
DAMNED LIES,
AND STATISTICS."

"IF HARD WORK WERE SUCH A WONDERFUL THING, SURELY THE RICH WOULD HAVE KEPT IT ALL TO THEMSELVES."

LANE KIRKLAND
AFL-CIO PRESIDENT

"THE HAPPIEST TIME
IN ANY MAN'S LIFE IS
WHEN HE IS IN RED-HOT
PURSUIT OF A DOLLAR
WITH A REASONABLE
PROSPECT OF
OVERTAKING IT."

JOSH BILLINGS

"EXPERIENCE
IS THE NAME
EVERYONE GIVES
TO THEIR
MISTAKES."

OSCAR WILDE

Maier's law:

"If the facts do not conform to the theory, they must be disposed of."

"BUY LOW, SELL HIGH, COLLECT EARLY, AND PAY LATE."

DICK LEVIN

"EVEN IF YOU'RE ON THE RIGHT TRACK, YOU'LL GET RUN OVER IF YOU JUST SIT THERE."

WILL ROGERS

"MANAGEMENT
IS THE ART OF
GETTING OTHER
PEOPLE TO DO
ALL THE WORK."

"I'D LIKE TO BE
RICH ENOUGH SO I
COULD THROW
SOAP AWAY AFTER
THE LETTERS ARE
WORN OFF."

ANDY ROONEY

"WHEN THEY SAY A MAN IS A 'BORN EXECUTIVE' THEY MEAN HIS FATHER OWNS THE BUSINESS."

"LET US BE THANKFUL FOR THE FOOLS. BUT FOR THEM THE REST OF US COULD NOT SUCCEED."

MARK TWAIN

"MONEY WON'T BUY
HAPPINESS, BUT IT WILL
PAY THE SALARIES OF A
LARGE RESEARCH STAFF
TO STUDY THE PROBLEM."

BILL VAUGHAN

The Success Collection

BY CELEBRATING EXCELLENCE

SUCCESSORIES LIBRARY

TOLL FREE (800) 535-2773
919 Springer Drive • Lombard, IL 60148